My Book About Clothes

Clothes are fun as well as useful! This colourful book uses big, bright photographs and simple words to describe the different kinds of clothes people wear – and why. It describes clothes for indoors and outdoors, for hot and cold weather, uniforms, sports clothes and clothes for dressing up. The words and pictures have been carefully chosen to develop reading skills and promote interest and discussion.

My Book About

The Body   Houses and Homes

Clothes   Toys

Food   Weather

Editor: Anna Girling
Designer: Loraine Hayes

First published in 1991 by
Wayland (Publishers) Ltd
61 Western Road, Hove
East Sussex BN3 1JD, England

British Library Cataloguing in Publication Data
Jackman, Wayne
My book about clothes. – (My book about)
I. Title   II. Series
428.4

ISBN 0 7502 0122 3

Typeset by Kalligraphic Design Ltd, Horley, Surrey
Printed and bound by Casterman S.A., Belgium

Words that are **underlined** in the text
are explained in the glossary on page 22.

My Book About Clothes

WAYNE JACKMAN

Wayland

Look at the
clothes this
girl is
wearing.
Her clothes
are very
colourful.

**Do you
like the
bright
colours?**

4

Here are some clothes laid out on a bed.
Do you have any clothes like these?

What do you put on first when you get dressed in the morning?

This girl is
getting dressed.
She is putting
on her jumper.

**What has she
got on her
T-shirt?**

6

Shoes go on last of all. This boy can tie up his own shoelaces.

Do your shoes have shoelaces?

Some clothes are for wearing indoors.
We wear slippers indoors.

Here are some funny slippers!
What do they have on them?

Some clothes are for wearing outdoors.

We wear rain clothes to keep us dry.
This girl is wearing a hat, a raincoat and boots.

What colours are her rain clothes?

In **winter** we wear warm clothes. Warm clothes keep out the cold. Even the snowman has a scarf!

What clothes are these children wearing to keep them warm?

In **summer** it is hot.
We do not need to wear lots of clothes.

We can wear shorts and a T-shirt.

Sometimes it is fun to wear unusual clothes.
These children are going to a fancy-dress party.
They have put on funny clothes.

What have they dressed up as?

Have you ever been to the **circus**? Circus **clowns** wear very colourful clothes.

Would you like to wear clothes like a clown?

This boy likes to ride his skateboard. He wears a **helmet**, elbow pads and gloves.

They stop him getting hurt if he falls over.

Painting can be messy.
An **overall** will stop your
clothes getting dirty.

**Have you got a
painting overall?**

Some people wear special clothes for their job. They are called **uniforms**. Have you ever seen a uniform like this?

Why do you think people wear uniforms?

These teams are playing American football.
Their uniforms help us to tell the teams apart.

Can you see the man wearing a striped shirt?

Many clothes are made of **wool**.
Do you know where wool comes from?

It comes from sheep.
Have you got a woollen jumper?

This girl's clothes are made of **cotton**. Cotton comes from a plant. It grows in hot, sunny countries. The girl is holding a cotton plant.

This person lives in a very hot **desert**.

He wears loose white clothes.
His clothes keep him cool.
What is he wearing on his feet?

This boy is in an
icy **igloo**.
Outside it is
very cold.
He needs to wear
thick clothes to
keep him warm.

**Can you see
the fur round
his hood?**

Glossary

Circus A show, held in a tent, with acrobats and clowns.

Clowns People who wear funny clothes and make people laugh.

Cotton Thin cloth that is often used for summer clothes.

Desert A place where few plants grow, usually because it is too hot and dry.

Helmet A kind of hard hat that protects your head.

Igloo A round-shaped house made of blocks of snow. The Innuit people who live near the cold North Pole make igloos as temporary homes.

Overall Something you wear over your clothes to keep them clean.

Summer The time of year when the weather is warmest.

Uniforms Special clothes that are all alike. People wear uniforms to show they are all part of the same group.

Winter The time of year when the weather is coldest.

Wool The thick hair on a sheep. It is made into thread for knitting or for making into cloth.

Books to read

Clothes by Gerald Hawksley
(Blackie, 1988)

Clothes by Jenny Vaughan
(Macdonald, 1987)

Costumes and Clothes by Jean
Cooke (Wayland, 1986)

Denim Jeans by Wayne
Jackman (Wayland, 1990)

Leather Shoes by Wayne
Jackman (Wayland, 1990)

My Jumper by Robert Pressling
(A & C Black, 1990)

Nylon Tracksuit by Wayne
Jackman (Wayland, 1990)

Plastic Raincoat by Wayne
Jackman (Wayland, 1990)

Wool by Annabelle Dixon (A & C
Black, 1988)

Woolly Hat by Wayne Jackman
(Wayland, 1990)

Picture acknowledgements

The publishers would like to thank the following for providing the photographs for this book: Chapel Studios 5, 6, 8; Eye Ubiquitous 7 (Yiorgos Nikiteas); PHOTRI 4, 13 (Vic Bider), 14, 19; Tony Stone Worldwide 11 (Jo Browne/Mick Smee), 17 (Chris Cole), 21 (P. H. Cornut); Topham Picture Source 16; Wayland Picture Library cover (Zul Mukhida); Tim Woodcock 18; Zefa 9, 10 (Kelly/Mooney), 12, 15 (H. Koelsch), 20 (Klaus Benser).

Index